The Rain In Spain
A Kid's Guide To Barcelona, Spain

Photography By John D. Weigand
Poetry By Penelope Dyan

Bellissima Publishing, LLC
Jamul, California
www.bellissimapublishing.com

copyright © 2011 by Penny D. Weigand and John D. Weigand

All rights reserved. No part of this book may be reproduced or transmitted in any form or by any means, electronic or mechanical, including photocopying, recording, or by any other means, or by any information or storage retrieval system, without permission from the publisher.

ISBN 978-1-935630-56-2

First Edition

To the magic of Barcelona...

The Rain In Spain
Bellissima Publishing, LLC

Introduction

Barcelona was founded as a Roman city and became the capital of the Counts of Barcelona. It merged with the Kingdom of Aragon, and became one of the most important cities of the Crown of Aragon. It was besieged several times during its history. Today, Barcelona is a major tourist attraction and is probably known best for the work of architect Antoni Gaudí, pictured on the cover of this book (la sagrada familia). Barcelona held the 1992 Summer Olympic Games, and is also the headquarters of the Union for the Mediterranean are located in Barcelona. There are also several places called placa de torro. (place of the bulls) where bull fights are held, and soccer is a revered sport. As the capital of Catalonia, Barcelona houses the seat of the Catalan government, known as the Generalitat de Catalunya. The city is also the capital of the Province of Barcelona and the Barcelonès comarca (shire).

Setting all that serious stuff aside, Barcelona is definitely a place where a kid can have fun. You can use the pages of this book to be creative and insert postcards, tickets, and other memorabilia you collect for yourself along the way. Have a big explore and be just like Christopher Columbus! Look through the pages of this book to see some of the things that you might see and do in Barcelona when you go there, or use your imagination for an imaginary exploration of this city, and photographer John D. Weigand and award winning author, attorney and former teacher, Penelope Dyan will take you on your very own trip (with them) through the pages of this book.

This is yet another book that is meant for kids, that will look great on your parent's coffee table.

The Rain In Spain
Bellissima Publishing, LLC

The Rain In Spain
A Kid's Guide To Barcelona, Spain

Photography By John D. Weigand
Poetry By Penelope Dyan

When you get to Barcelona you can take a walk down the street.

Or you can hop on a tour bus
to save your weary feet.

You can see buildings with orange spirals.

You can see a reflecting pond
with a beautiful work of art.
And you can learn a lot about Spain's people,
if you are sharp and smart.

You can walk down a line of shops,
where the interesting stuff never stops.

You can see works of art just everywhere,
and it's okay to stop and stare.
You can have an artist sketch a picture of you,
if that is something you'd like to do.

You can see an artist painting something blue,
that you can purchase when he is through.

You can see a man with a skeleton on a bike,
as up along Rambla Street you take a hike.

And whether it's raining or it is sunny,
you can ALWAYS pat THIS fat clown's tummy.

If you are hungry you could eat this guy's head,
although you COULD have escargot instead.
In fact (of those) you could gather a pail,
because as you know an escargot is SNAIL!

If you had a kitchen you could cook raw meat.
But you'd probably prefer a pastry sweet.

Here is something that could meet your needs,
IF you had TIME to plant AND to grow seeds.
BECAUSE on Rambla Street you can find
seeds, plants and flowers of MANY a kind.
In fact, you can find EVERYTHING there!
(You can EVEN buy new UNDERWEAR!)

And then you're finally at McDonald's!
And your weary Mom can rest her feet!
And you are ready to have something
(other than slippery, slimy snails) to EAT!
And so you have a burger, a soda, some fries!
You rub your tummy with contentment,
a smile's in your eyes.

Because today you saw an AWFULLY lot!
You even saw a man sitting on a POT!
(Of course your dad thought it was VERY funny,
and your mom said it just proved SOME people
would do ANYTHING for money.)
But when it is all over, and all is said and done,
you will tell everyone you know
that YOU had an AWFUL LOT of fun.
And as Christopher Columbus points
to the Americas---through the blue of the sky
you will all know it is time
to say, "Adios! AND Good bye!"

"Following the light of the sun, we left the Old World."
Christopher Columbus